KABBALAH

By
Oracle Claretta Pam

Kabbalah

Oracle Claretta Pam

SACRED**VISION**
PRESS

Kabbalah

ISBN-10: 1-4913-1968-2   ISBN-13: 978-1-4913-1968-0 Paperback
ISBN-10: 1-4913-1969-0   ISBN-13: 978-1-4913-1969-7 Hardback
ISBN-10: 1-4913-1970-4   ISBN-13: 978-1-4913-1970-3 Kindle
ISBN-10: 1-4913-1971-2   ISBN-13: 978-1-4913-1971-0 iBook
ISBN-10: 1-4913-1972-0   ISBN-13: 978-1-4913-1972-7 Nook
ISBN-10: 1-4913-1973-9   ISBN-13: 978-1-4913-1973-4 AudioBook

Library of Congress Cataloging-in-Publication Data

Pam, Oracle Claretta.
  Kabbalah / Oracle Claretta Pam. -- First edition.
     p. cm.
  ISBN 1-4913-1968-2 (pb : alk. paper) -- ISBN 1-4913-1969-0 (hd : alk. paper) --
ISBN 1-4913-1973-9 (audiobk.) -- ISBN 1-4913-1970-4 (ebook) -- ISBN 1-4913-
1971-2 (ebook) -- ISBN 1-4913-1972-0 (ebook)
  1. Cabala. I. Title.
  BM526.P36 2014
  296.1'6--dc23
                          2014007577

          10 9 8 7 6 5 4 3 2 1   14 15 16 17 18

An interpretation of the printing code: is the number of the books printing. The rightmost number of the second series of numbers is
the year of the books printing. For example, a printing code of 1–14 shows that the first printing occurred in 2014.

First edition. August 2014

DEDICATION

To everyone and
everything in this universe.

Kabbalah

Most sacred vision books are available at special quantity discounts for bulk purchases first sales promotions, premiums, fundraising, or educational use. Special books, or book excerpts, can be created to fit specific needs. For details, email info@innovative-publishers.com.

Upcoming titles:
Agnosticism Atheism Non-Religion
Bahai Faith
Buddhism
Cao Dai
Catholicism
Christianity
Confucianism
Hinduism
Humanism
Islam
Jainism
Jehovas Witnesses
Juche North Korea
Judaism
Natural Law
Neopaganism
New Age
Primal Faith
Primal Indigenous
Rastafarianism
Scientology
Shinto
Sikhism
Spiritism
Taoism
Tarahumara Beliefs
Tenrikyo
The Occult
African Traditional - Diasporic
Unificationism
Unitarian Universalism
Zoroastrianism

CONTENTS

ACKNOWLEDGMENTS

A special note of thanks to the congregation at the Universal Life Church Monastery of Massachusetts both online and on the ground. Your encouragement and participation and spreading the understanding of all belief systems is what will effect positive change in this world and beyond.

I

Introduction to Kabbalah

Commonly perceived as a form of ancient Jewish mysticism, Kabbalah has become the center of widespread public attention in recent years—owing largely to its increasing popularity among famous celebrities in the entertainment industry, who perhaps seem to have turned the once exclusive and sacred esoteric tradition into the latest highly publicized Hollywood trend. Despite the recent celebrity fascination with it, Kabbalah is one of the oldest religious disciplines of the world whose origins are believed by some Kabbalists to in fact predate the major world religions of today.

Deriving its roots from the Hebrew term *"kibel,"* meaning *"to receive,"* Kabbalah is understood to be a received tradition which originally emerged as an integral part of Judaism based on the secret teachings about God and the universe, transcending traditional

1

Jewish theological beliefs. As such, it comprises a set of mystical, esoteric beliefs that seek to unveil the hidden knowledge pertaining to the ontological questions about our existence and spirituality, which have been passed down through generations, as a means to attain spiritual fulfillment.

Over the centuries, Kabbalah has developed from an early mystical Jewish tradition in the 12th century, to a contemporary system of spirituality today that continues to draw followers from various Jewish denominations as well as a number of non-Jewish adherents across the globe, giving rise to several different modern interpretations and adaptations of the ancient tradition that are currently practiced worldwide.

Origins and early history

Despite the origins of Kabbalah commonly being traced back to the late 12th century in Medieval Spain and Europe, the question of its actual birth has long been subject to uncertainty and debate amongst researchers and historians—particularly due to the limited number of authentic primary sources and historical literature that are available for study today, rendering much of its early history inaccessible. One of the earliest known Kabbalistic texts, titled *Sefer HaBashir*, for instance, is seemingly addressed to a readership that is assumed to be already well-versed in its language and terminology, indicating existence of preceding texts and writings from before. A handful of certain ancient Jewish mystical texts that have been preserved, on the other hand, date back as early as the 1st or 2nd century CE, making them virtually incomprehensible to scholars today.

A major reason behind the lost writings of antiquity that have led to the resulting difficulty in tracing the exact birth of the Kabbalah may perhaps be the strict adherence to secrecy amongst early Kabbalists, which prohibited them from recording the esoteric teachings in writing form. As such, the ancient mystical teachings of Kabbalah had traditionally been passed down from generations of masters, prophets and sages to their disciples primarily through oral communication. The reluctance to print written texts of Kabbalistic teachings may also have stemmed from the difficultly in expressing divine mystical experiences through language, due to its many limitations. Nahmanides—one of the earliest and most prominent scholars of Kabbalah—has stated that despite the existence of early Kabbalistic texts, their true message could only be understood if it was imparted by the teacher orally to the student, so as to prevent any miscommunication or misinterpretation of the teachings.

Followers of Kabbalah generally regard the ancient mystical tradition as preceding all organized religious systems of the world and essentially trace its origins to the first revelations of God to Adam. As such, the sacred knowledge of Kabbalah is believed to have been transmitted to mankind in three distinct stages, with Adam marking the first human being to receive the teachings through the Archangel Raziel.

The second revelation is understood to be received four thousand years ago by Abraham—the Patriarch of Judaism, forefather of Christianity and one of the earliest prophets of Islam. Abraham's

Covenant with God is said to have contained the sacred knowledge of Kabbalah, which he transcribed in *Sefer Yetzirah*, The Book of Formation—the earliest surviving text on Jewish mysticism today.

The third revelation was given to Moses—a prominent prophet of Judaism, Christianity, Islam and several other major religions of the world. It is believed that Moses received the sacred knowledge of Kabbalah from God at Mount Sinai in the 13th century BCE, which thus formed a significant part of the Oral Torah, being passed on *"by word of mouth"* through generations.

In its early stages, Kabbalah is believed to have been openly practiced in ancient Israel around the 10th Century CE, but its rising popularity soon began to threaten the established religious system of the time and eventually exposed its followers to the dangers of being exiled and persecuted for their association with the mystical tradition. As a result, Kabbalists ultimately concealed their sacred knowledge within cryptic esoteric symbols in order to safeguard themselves from the threat of persecution and protect their teachings from being distorted and corrupted through an unsupervised practice, misuse and exploitation of the divine tradition. Kabbalah thus became a highly secretive esoteric school of thought, being practically lost in obscurity for the following two and a half centuries.

3

The rise of Kabbalah in the Middle Ages

It was not until the late 12th century that Kabbalah began to reemerge in Medieval Europe and Spain, with a rise in the number of mystical fraternities that formed following the increasing influence of various *Rishonim* who were the leading rabbis of Kabbalah at the time. Nahmanides—popularly known as *Ramban*—was a prominent Medieval rabbi and Kabbalist who composed a commentary on the *Torah* based on the teachings of Kabbalah during this period which went on to become his most well-known work.

Another eminent Kabbalist of the time was Moses de Leon—a Spanish rabbi who, in the year 1270 CE, discovered what is believed to be the most sacred work of literature in Kabbalah: the *Zohar*. Regarded by followers as the leading authoritative Kabbalistic text, the book of *Zohar* was brought to light by Moses de Leon after nine hundred years of being lost and hidden from the world. Despite the exact date of its composition and question of authorship being generally disputed amongst the Kabbalist community, the *Zohar* is widely believed to have been composed by the famous rabbinic sage, Simeon bar Yochai, between the 2nd and 3rd centuries. Through the *Zohar*, the influence of Kabbalah soon began to spread across the region, attracting a number of followers.

The Lurianic Kabbalah

Following the Jewish expulsion from Spain in the year 1492, Kabbalah spread, along with its exiled adherents, to the Balkans, Italy and Israel. By the mid-sixteenth century, several distinguished mystics and scholars of Kabbalah had settled in Safed—a city in Galilee, Israel—sparking off what is believed to constitute the 16th century renaissance of Kabbalah. It was during this period that Kabbalah began to be widely studied and Safed rapidly became the center of Jewish mystical wisdom, aided by the influence of renowned mystics and thinkers—particularly the Jewish Rabbi, Isaac Luria, popularly known as the *Ari* ("the Holy Lion").

Perhaps the most influential thinkers in the history of Kabbalah, the *Ari* was a gifted thinker who explored the depths of the *Zohar* and revolutionized Kabbalah by presenting a new interpretation of the sacred text. He was soon embraced by the Kabbalist community as a prominent master of the divine mystical tradition, and spent the last three years of his life immersed in the development and explanation of

Kabbalah. After his death, the *Ari's* teachings were compiled by his students and titled "*The Writings of the Ari,*" which led to the birth of a new and advanced form of Kabbalistic thought, known as the *Lurianic* Kabbalah, being thus named after him. *Lurianic* Kabbalah expounded new principles of the origins of Creation, unveiling hidden meanings within the sacred teachings and soon established itself as the definitive basis for Kabbalistic thought up until this day.

4

Later Kabbalist movements

Despite significant political and economic changes in the region that adversely impacted the Kabbalist community in Safed, the mystical teachings continued to attract new followers with the rise of several movements that began to emerge at the hands of popular Kabbalist teachers in the 17th and 18th centuries. One such movement was started by Shabbati Zevi—a controversial Kabbalist teacher— who claimed to be the promised Jewish Messiah, whose coming had been foretold in the Jewish Bible. His movement soon began to attract a mass following and became known as the Jewish Sabbatean movement. The movement, however, was short-lived, as Zevi was arrested by the Ottoman ruler and ultimately converted to Islam in order to escape persecution, thus becoming an apostate to Judaism.

Following the chaos that ensued, the rabbis prohibited the public teaching of Kabbalah thereafter and the mystical tradition once again fell into secrecy, becoming subject to strict restrictions.

As a result, a number of Kabbalist teachers remained hidden and commonly formed underground *"circles"*. One such circle continued to impart the teachings of Rabbi Isaac Luria for the next two centuries in Eastern Europe and by 1740, a teacher from among them decided to make these teachings available to the public in Ukraine. This teacher was known as *Baal Shem Tov* (the "Master of the Good Name")—an influential rabbi and mystic of the time who founded the movement of *Hasidic* Judaism. The followers of *Hasidic* Judaism were called *Hasidim* ("the Devout Ones") and the movement—which triggered as a response to highly restrictive nature of traditional Jewish thought—was based on promoting unity and brotherhood through the love of God, by highlighting the spiritual bond between every member of the Jewish community, irrespective of their rabbinic expertise or scholarly knowledge. *Hasidic* Judaism went on to influence a number of Jews in Eastern Europe, drawing more people to pursue the teachings of Kabbalah.

By the late-nineteenth century, the Jewish community in Russia began to suffer great persecution, which ultimately led to the decline of Jewish mysticism. Furthermore, the 20th century Holocaust issued by Nazi Germany during World War II, led to the ensuing massacre of millions of Jews in Europe, which included a majority of the rabbis who also lost their lives. The *Hasidic* teachings, however, still managed to survive through a handful of Kabbalist masters and soon began to spread to the United

States, following a wave of migrations.

During the 1970's, the Jewish Renewal Movement began to gain momentum, attracting scores of Jews in several cities to participate in it and promote the study of Jewish mysticism and other religious and spiritual traditions of Judaism. As a result, a number of Jewish traditions began to incorporate mysticism into their teachings, soon drawing the interest of several non-Jews who were particularly captivated by the teachings of Kabbalah.

The 21ˢᵗ century has witnessed an unprecedented rise in the popularity of Kabbalah, most notably through the mass media, at the hands of numerous well-known celebrities who have publically embraced its teachings in recent years, leading to various present-day New Age and Occultist interpretations of the ancient mystical tradition.

5

The three divisions of Kabbalah

The study of Kabbalah is essentially divided on the basis of three separate distinctions, each of which, are distinguished by their underlying intent and purpose in relation to God and consequently centered on the areas of wisdom, action and devotion, respectively. The three basic "models" or branches of Kabbalah are thus classified as Theoretical Kabbalah, Practical Kabbalah and Meditative Kabbalah.

Theoretical Kabbalah

Also referred to as Kabbalah *Iyunit*, Theoretical Kabbalah is based on the theosophical tradition of the mystical teachings and as such, seeks to impart the wisdom and philosophy of Kabbalah and explain it. The study of the *Zohar* constitutes an integral part of Theoretical Kabbalah, which presents the basic conceptual framework that contains all the theological ideas underlying Kabbalistic teachings. The study of the *Torah* also plays an instrumental role in the practice of this tradition as a means to understand the central concepts of Kabbalah, such as the *Tree of Life* and the Nature of the Divine. Theoretical Kabbalah thus explains the process of creation with respect to the infinite will of God and explores the nature of the relationship between God and His creation through the ten *sefirot*.

Theoretical Kabbalah is fundamentally rooted in *Lurianic* Kabbalah—the Kabbalistic thought founded by 16th century rabbi, Isaac Luria or the *Ari*, who is widely regarded as "the father" of contemporary Kabbalah. Luria's teachings presented a deeper and more comprehensive interpretation of the *"true meaning"* of the *Zohar* and largely contributed to shaping and influencing Theoretical Kabbalah, which is predominantly studied worldwide as the leading Kabbalistic tradition today, having laid down the basic guidelines for the rest of the Kabbalistic traditions to follow. It is thus through Theoretical Kabbalah, that Practical and Meditative Kabbalah can be practiced and understood.

Practical Kabbalah

Practical Kabbalah comprises the theurgical tradition of Kabbalistic teachings that is based on the practice of magical acts and rituals as a means to influence reality and alter the Divine universe and the physical world. These practices primarily involve the summoning of spiritual forces and angelic entities through the incantation of Divine Names for the purpose of benefiting the creation and furthering the Divine plan, by reaching a collective realization of the ultimate Divine purpose for all creation.

Generally regarded as a form of pure "white" magic, Practical Kabbalah—also known as Kabbalah *Ma'asit*—originated as a highly esoteric tradition, whose practice was initially confined to an extremely secretive, exclusive circle of seasoned and elite masters due to their piety and proximity to God, which distinguished them from those who had not reached the requisite state of purity necessary for participating in it. Engaging in the practice of Kabbalistic magic by those who were impure was believed to be inevitably destructive to both, the practitioners, as well as everyone involved in the act, and as such, it was strictly prohibited to anyone outside of the sacred circles due to its countless dangers.

Practical Kabbalah later evolved through the Temple service of ritual cleansing that began to be offered in ancient Jerusalem, which enabled one to purify oneself from the impurity resulting from contact with the other world through death, when delving into the practice of magic. The service, which was offered in the Temple of Solomon, allowed one to obtain purity through the ashes of the red heifer and involved the incantation of the Divine Names by the High Priest on the day of *Yom Kippur*—the Day of Atonement. The central component of this service comprised the recitation of the most sacred essential Name of God,

"*Havayah*," whose utterance was forbidden outside of the Temple.

The incantations and enunciations of Divine Names that were employed in the Temple Service followed an extremely precise method and technique, which was passed down through several generations. By the time of the Second Temple, the mystics and rabbis began to conceal their sacred methods out of increasing fears of their practices falling into the wrong "unworthy" hands and thereby corrupting them. Following the destruction of the Second Temple, the sacred rituals of Practical Kabbalah were gradually forgotten.

In the later centuries, Practical Kabbalah was revived through Talmudic and Gaonic influences, particularly, the tradition of *Merkabah* Mysticism—an ancient form of Jewish mysticism based on the attainment of the Throne of God through the magical incantations of Divine Names for the purpose of spiritual ascent.

In the 13th century, *Hasidic* Ashkenazi Jews were drawn to the idea of *golum*—the creation of artificial life by means of Divine invocations and magic. Inspired by the esoteric teachings of the *Sefir Yetzirah* regarding the creative force of certain letters of the Hebrew alphabet, they incorporated this practice into Practical Kabbalah.

It was not until the Middle Ages, however, that

the distinction between Practical and Theoretical Kabbalah began to emerge, following the strict prohibition of the practices and rituals associated with Practical Kabbalah by a number of prominent traditional Kabbalists such as Abraham Abulafia and most notably, Isaac Luria (the *Ari*)—one of the central figures of authority on Kabbalistic knowledge—who strongly disapproved of such practices and thereby condemned them. These masters asserted that without the Holy Temple and the ritual cleansing service it used to offer, it was impossible to achieve the requisite state of purity required for the pursuit of Practical Kabbalah and as such, began to replace the practice of magic with meditative and conceptual techniques. Luria, for instance, developed a pure form of exorcism that displaced magical rites and rituals with meditative exercises centered on faith, as opposed to magic, and deemed the pursuit of Practical Kabbalah *"demeaning to the soul"*.

18th century rabbi and mystic, *Baal Shem Tov* was a prominent healer of the time who used meditative and psychic exercises that commonly employed the use of amulets inscribed with the Names of God, which were worn by his followers for the purpose of protection and healing. However, he later abandoned this practice and instead of inscribing Divine Names on the amulets, he began writing his own name, thus transmitting Divine light and blessings directly from his own soul.

Baal Shem Tov disregarded many of his previous

practices later in his life and alternatively began stressing upon the power of pure faith by turning to a more internalized form of mysticism, which formed the basis of *Hasidic* Judaism. This mystical doctrine emphasized the ability of an individual soul to influence the universe directly through its connection to God, based solely on love and devotion. He thus introduced the philosophy of *deveikut*—the practice of "cleaving to God"—into the *Hasidic* school by integrating it with the concept of clinging to the *tzaddik*—the pious and righteous *Hasidic Rebbe* (Spiritual Master). Attachment to the *tzaddik* was a central component of the *Hasidic* teachings, whereby the *tzaddik* served as manifestations and channels of the Divine spiritual blessings flowing through them, to their disciples. By engaging in this practice, the *tzaddik* altered the Divine will by realizing a deeper will through their own spiritual proximity to God and self-sacrifice.

However, due to many great *tzaddik* being well known for their powerful supernatural abilities at the time, a number of people were drawn to the art of alchemy, healing, divination, astrology and other forms of practical magic. While a majority of the traditional Kabbalist rabbis and masters later prohibited the pursuit of Practical Kabbalah, the early masters firmly restricted its practice to the true *tzaddik* whose ability stemmed from a positive, Divine source. They warned of the dangers of anyone else practicing it by stressing that a practitioner who is not a *tzaddik* would inevitably channel powers stemming from a combination of light and darkness and its final result would ultimately always be negative.

As a result, much of these practices soon began to deviate from their pure, original teachings and guidelines and eventually proved the fears of the ancient masters to be true, as occult influences began to creep into Practical Kabbalah. The following centuries witnessed a massive increase in pseudo-Kabbalist movements centered on the distortion of the sacred practices taught by the ancient masters, which often employed the use of dark and impure magic through desecration of the Divine. Thus emerged the tradition known as Hermetic *Qaballah*, which constituted the underlying philosophy for a number of occult, esoteric movements and secret societies that came forth in the modern era, including the likes of the Golden Dawn, the Fellowship of the Rosy Cross and most notably, the *Thelemic* order founded by 20th century Western occultist and ceremonial magician, Aleister Crowley. Hermetic *Qabbalah* also played a significant role in influencing the Wiccan, Neopagan and New Age movements.

In contrast with the ancient Kabbalist masters, a number of the occult magicians—particularly those belonging to the Left-Hand Path—traced the source of their practices to the *Qliphoth* realm of evil which manifests the impure spiritual forces in Judaism and represents the *"other side"* of holiness. By using an inverted desecration of the ten holy *sefirot*, the practitioners sought the aid of demonic and satanic entities to perform their black magic rituals.

Despite constituting a blatant distortion of the authentic Kabbalistic teachings and sharing virtually nothing in common with them, many of these movements and the practices associated with them soon began to threaten the reputation of Kabbalah, generating increasing criticism and skepticism regarding its philosophy and ultimately causing it to become perhaps one of the most misunderstood religious traditions of today.

As a result, Practical Kabbalah has essentially been shunned by a majority of today's traditional Kabbalists, as instructed by the ancient masters. Despite its practice once being Divinely favored at the hands of the "worthy," *Baal Shem Tov*, along with other eminent Kabbalist masters, saw no use for Practical Kabbalah any longer and attributed its lack of need and purpose in the world to the impending Messianic Age or the end of times, symbolizing humanity's evolved potential to reach an even greater and more elevated state of consciousness. He asserted that within this Age, the miraculous and magical will cease to inspire awe and ultimately become a natural part of life, while the secret and esoteric will, in turn, become common knowledge. He thus taught that the only means to purify our souls and reconnect with the Divine in these times is by connecting ourselves to the *tzadikim* who embody the Divinely guided, pure souls of the generation.

Meditative Kabbalah

Meditative Kabbalah is centered on the practice of a systematic series of meditations, prayers and spiritual exercises as a means to elevate the soul and access higher energies, in order to achieve Divine Union with God. Much of these meditative practices and exercises include the recitation of the Divine Names of God in Judaism, various combinations of letters of the Hebrew alphabet, *kavanah* (mystical intentions) and the adherence to the *mitzvah*—the 613 commandments of God ordained upon His creation in Judaism.

Also referred to as "Ecstatic Kabbalah," Meditative Kabbalah takes its roots from Prophetic Kabbalah—the Kabbalistic tradition established by 13th century Kabbalist and rabbi, Abraham Abulafia. Through Prophetic Kabbalah, Abulafia established an alternative to Theoretical Kabbalah and laid down the foundations for much of the meditative techniques that were later incorporated into Meditative Kabbalah. Drawing upon the teachings of *Sefer Yetzirah* (the Book of Formation), Prophetic Kabbalah was primarily focused on the attainment of Divine Union through the *"Kabbalah of Names"*—a series of complex combinations of Divine Names and letters of the Hebrew alphabet—for the purpose of reaching the ultimate spiritual or "prophetic" state, similar to the one experienced by prophets and sages, known as "Prophetic Kabbalah." However, some early Kabbalists attributed certain meditative practices to practical Kabbalah and thereby prohibited them, as a result of which, a vast majority of Abulafia's writings were never officially published and have thus only survived in the form of manuscript.

Meditative Kabbalah was later expanded through the teachings of Isaac Luria, who developed an extensive system of meditative practices drawn from the *Zohar*, called *Yichudim*, meaning "Unifications." These practices were based on the *Lurianic* scheme of Kabbalah and thus focused on the interaction of the *partzufim*—a reconfiguration of the ten Divine emanations or *sefirot* of Kabbalah.

The 18th century founder of *Hassidic* Judaism, *Baal Shem Tov*, also contributed to Meditative Kabbalah by incorporating psychological exercises centered on the Divine through envisioning His Names and entering the supernal universes contained in them. These visualization exercises would often induce high states of ecstasy and became integrated into the system of *Hasidism*.

Over the years, Meditative Kabbalah has evolved into an eclectic mix of numerous different meditative techniques and prayers, ranging from the Eastern as well as Western traditions. As a result, it is commonly met with a great deal of skepticism, however, the ancient traditional Kabalistic Meditation as taught by its masters is regarded as an important part of Kabbalah by providing the practical groundwork for its teachings. Furthermore, by presenting what may be described as a milder, simpler and moderate form of Practical Kabbalah that is in accordance with the sacred texts and teachings of Kabbalah, Meditative Kabbalah serves as the middle ground between Theoretical and Practical Kabbalah and harmonizes the teachings with their practice in a balanced way.

6

The beliefs and teachings of Kabbalah

Being generally associated with esoteric Jewish mysticism, Kabbalah is composed of sacred mystical teachings that contain wisdom about the hidden and unknown secrets of our universe. This ancient wisdom—being largely transmitted orally through generations, conforming to a strict traditional code of secrecy—is essentially centered on a basic fundamental belief that in fact underlies virtually all the major monotheistic religions of the world: The belief in a single, Omnipotent and Eternal God. 12th century rabbi, Maimonides, summed up this belief in the in the following words of the *Mishneh* Torah, that are often quoted by traditional Kabbalists to describe the wisdom of Kabbalah:

"The foundation of all foundations and the pillar of all wisdom is to know that there is God who brought into being all existence. All the beings of the heavens, and the earth, and what is between them came into existence only from the truth of God's being."

—*Mishneh Torah* (1:1)

From this central belief stem the basic teachings and concepts underlying Kabbalah.

7

The nature of God

The primary principle of Kabbalistic teachings holds that the world *"as we see it"* is not real. Contrary to other religions which regard the world as an illusion, Kabbalah instead considers human beings—in their limited capacity—as physically incapable of seeing it in its "real" and complete form. Since the real world lies beyond the ability of our senses to perceive, it constitutes a part of a much greater, infinite reality that exists within God and is referred to by Kabbalists as *"Ein Sof"* (The Infinite). As such, every human feeling, emotion and experience is a manifestation of the traits and attributes of God and serves as a reflection of one or more of His Divine characteristics. Kabbalists thus perceive God as the pinnacle of perfection and the totality of all that exists in the universe, while His creation simply reflects different aspects of His Nature.

Since everything that exists, descends from the same Divine source, what we as human beings perceive is merely a partial and imperfect image of the whole that actually exists in its complete, pure and perfect form inside this source, which is God. Kabbalists view God as *"the sum of all perfections"* and thereby believe that the ultimate purpose of all human beings is to identify all the worldly traces of His perfections and follow them back to their original Source, thus attaining the true form of Reality.

At the same time, God is considered a mystery, being described as *"That Which Is Without End"* and He is therefore ultimately believed to be unknowable and unreachable, transcending all bounds of human imagination and perception. However, since the universe and everything that exists within it was created by God and inherently exists within Him, Kabbalists believe that despite our inability to know God, it is still possible to experience mystical oneness with His Being through His creation. Renowned Medieval Kabbalist and rabbi, Moses de Leon, has described the unity of *The Infinite* as *"the chain of being"* that connects everything, *"from the highest to the lowest, extending from the upper pool to the edge of the universe"*. He has expressed this *chain of being* in the following words:

"God is one, God's secret is one, all the worlds below and above are all mysteriously one. Divine existence is indivisible. The entire chain is one. Down to the last link, everything is linked with everything else; so Divine essence is below as well as above, in heaven and on earth. There is nothing else."

Since all of God's creation are a part of His Divine Being, everything that exists within and around us are fragments of His attributes—including even human sexuality itself—which is, in essence, rooted in Divine sexuality. The human sexuality, which defines the male and female gender and characteristics, is inherently present within God, in whose Being, both the male and female dimensions exist in a state of perfect balance and harmony. At the same time, God cannot be confined to a certain gender or be described in terms of it, as His Being is limitless and infinite, wherein all the Divine attributes are unified in a complete and absolute state of perfection.

As such, it is the overabundance of these characteristics—for instance the level of masculinity or femininity—or alternatively, the insufficiency and lack of them, that results in conflict, stemming from the imbalance of the male and female energies.

One may then argue that since every human trait is a reflection of the attributes of the Divine, it must, by definition, also include the negative side of human emotions and attributes, or the lower and "base" human instincts and feelings. However, Kabbalists perceive God as an omnipotent entity, in whose Being, all of the Divine traits and attributes find perfect union and harmony and although these attributes are mirrored in His creation, they are imperfect and lacking, resulting in disharmony and polarization. Thus, the negative aspects of our existence are defined by Kabbalists in terms of the positive, for instance, by understanding darkness as the absence of light, or hatred as the absence of love.

Since human beings are created in the image of God, Kabbalists believe that everyone on earth is born inherently good and it is therefore the imbalance of the divine attributes through which the "negative" (or dark side of) human emotions are born out of. Similarly, the excessive overindulgence of certain human instincts— for instance the sexual drive—or the extreme suppression of them, may lead to conflict. Kabbalists thus believe that human beings possess the ability to restore the natural balance of the divine attributes within them by constantly seeking to emulate the Source of these attributes and living life in moderation.

8

The 10 Sefirot and the Tree of Life

At the heart of sacred Kabbalistic teachings lies the concept of the *sefirot*. Derived from the Hebrew term *saper*, meaning "to tell," the word *sefirot* is translated as "emanations." As such, the *sefirot* refer to the ten Divine emanations, through which, the *Ein Sof*—the Hidden God—has revealed Himself to His creation. Commonly known as the ten stages, pillars or *"inner faces"* of God, the *sefirot* are composed of the ten names of God—each reflecting a different Divine aspect or attribute—and are traditionally represented by the sacred symbol of the *Tree of Life*, which is also the universally recognized official symbol of Kabbalah.

Despite originally being introduced in the *Sefir Yetzirah* (the Book of Formation)—the oldest surviving text on Jewish mysticism—the concept of the *sefirot*, along with the rest of the teachings contained in the *Sefir Yetzirah*, are believed to have been revealed to Abraham long ago, who passed the sacred wisdom on to his sons.

Each of the ten *sefirah* constitutes a separate and distinct way of perceiving and knowing God, being thus described by the 18th century Kabbalist, Rabbi Moses Luzzatto, as the ten *"veils"* that lie between God and His creation and serve as *"channels through which His bounty might be transmitted to man"*. Despite God being perceived as a hidden mystery who is ultimately unknowable and unattainable, through the *sefirot,* His infinite Glory is unified within a finite number, being *"so densified that the lower creations could bear it"*.

The oneness of the Hidden God and His emanations is stressed upon in the *Zohar,* which states that the *Ein Sof* and the *sefirot* are in fact a part of the same *"lamp"* whose *"lights spread out on every side"* through His emanations, but upon examining these lights, we discover *"that only the lamp itself exists"*. Much like the Christian concept of the Holy Trinity that is composed of three, the *sefirot,* too, contain ten Divine manifestations which are thus unified in a single infinite God.

The union of the ten *sefirot* is embodied in the *Tree of Life*—a symbolic arrangement of the ten Divine names, depicting *"a complex pattern of emanation"* through which God reveals Himself to His creation. As such, the ten *sefirot* trace their roots from the Hidden *Ein Sof,* out of which, the first emanation is born, known as *Keter*—the "Crown" of the *sefirot.* From *Keter* emanate *Hokhmah* (Wisdom) and *Binah*

(Understanding), which come together with *Keter* to form the upper triad. It is from the upper *sefirot* that the seven lower *sefirot* are generated, which are composed of *Hesed* (Love/Kindness), *Gevurah* (Justice), *Tiferet* (Beauty), *Netzah* (Victory), *Hod* (Splendor), *Yesod* (Foundation) and *Malkhut* (Kingdom), also known as *Shekhinah* (Divine Feminine).

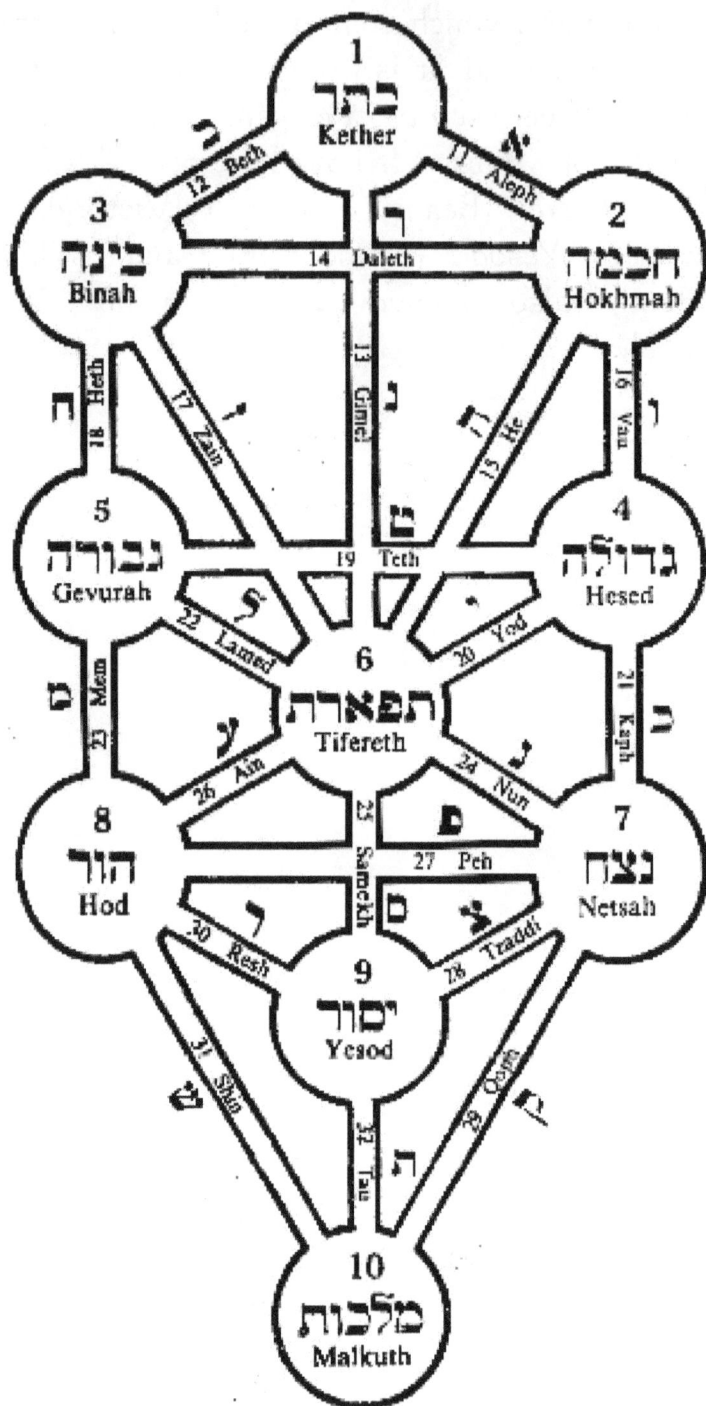

9

The First Triad

1- *Keter*: The highest *sefirah* on the *Tree of Life*, *Keter* means "Crown," being described in the *Zohar* as *"the most hidden of all hidden things"* due to its proximity to the *Ein Sof*. Being the first *sefirah*, *Keter* represents the manifestation of the *"infinite will"* of God, often referred to as the *"Hidden Light"* that is regarded by some Kabbalists as inconceivable and in comprehensible to the human mind. At the same time, despite existing within the *Ein Sof*, *Keter* is generally distinguished from it, symbolizing *"the catalyst of all being, but yet a thing in itself"*.

2- *Hokhmah*: The second *sefirah* on the *Tree of Life*, *Hokhmah* is translated as "Wisdom" and represents the primal stage of creation. Despite being the second *sefirah*, it is often referred to as the *"Beginning"* which represents *"the first ray of divine light"* emanating from *Keter*, the *"unknowable"*. Being described in the *Zohar* as the embodiment of *"divine thought"*, *Hokhmah* is believed to contain the sacred blueprint and design for all creation. *Hokhmah* is also regarded as the archetype of the masculine and is commonly known as *"Abba"*, which is Hebrew for father, thus symbolizing the *"Father of all creation"*.

3- *Binah:* The third *sefirah* of the upper triad,
Binah means "Understanding" and
represents the feminine Nature of God, being
referred to as *Imma* or the Divine Mother.
Thus, together, *Hokhmah* and *Binah* embody
the parents of all creation, from whom the
seven lower *Sefirot* are born. As such, *Binah*
symbolizes the "womb" of the Divine Mother
and along with *Keter* and *Hokhmah,*
constitutes the head of the human body.

10

The Second Triad

4- *Hesed:* Commonly translated as "Love" or "Mercy," *Hesed* is the fourth *sefirah* which stems from *Binah* and is also sometimes referred to as *Gedullah* (Greatness). *Hesed* symbolizes *"the right hand of God",* representing unconditional love and kindness, and marks the birth of emotional energy in the stages of creation. Being a central virtue in Judaism, *Hesed* is also associated with Abraham.

5- *Gevurah:* The fifth *sefirah* of the *Tree of Life, Gevurah* is translated as "Justice" or "Severity" and is often referred to as *Din* (Judgment). *Gevurah* represents the left arm or shoulder of God and serves as a manifestation of His judgment, being associated with Isaac—the son of Abraham. Just like the complimentary relationship between *Hokhmah* and *Binah, Gevurah* and *Hesed,* too, represent two opposite sides of the same Divine personality. As such, the severity of Justice, Power and Judgment stemming from *Gevurah* is mitigated by finding balance and harmony with the Loving Kindness and Mercy of *Hesed.* Similarly, the extreme overabundance of Mercy without restraint poses dangers and is thus controlled by the contracting nature of Justice and Judgment through *Gevurah,* creating a necessary balance in the universe.

6- *Tiferet:* Sitting at the center of the *Tree of Life* is *Tiferet,* the sixth *sefirah,* which means "Beauty". It is out of the harmonious union between *Hesed's* Love and Mercy and *Gevurah's* Judgment that *Tiferet's* Beauty is born, which is also referred to as *Rahamim,* meaning "Compassion". *Tiferet* symbolizes the center of God's chest and represents integration and balance by mediating the opposing energies of *Hesed* and *Gevurah.* *Tiferet* is described in the *Zohar* as *"the Son"* who has *"been crowned with judgment and compassion"* and *"the mighty tree, whose head reaches toward heaven and whose head is rooted in the holy ground".* It is also associated with Jacob—the son of Isaac—who has been referred to in the *Zohar* as *"the center bar in the middle of the planks",* alluding to the center of *Tree of Life,* that is, *Tiferet.* *Tiferet* thus represents the masculine aspect of God and is also referred to as *"the King".*

II

The *Third Triad and the final sefirah*

7- *Netzah:* The seventh *sefirah* of the *Tree of Life, Netzah* is translated as "Victory" and symbolizes the right leg of God. *Netzah* represents endurance, eternity and the infinite mercy of God, being regarded as the lower manifestation of *Hesed* (Love/Mercy), and is essentially characterized by formless spiritual energy. It is also associated with Moses and reflects his Divine authority over the Israelites.

8- *Hod:* Sitting across *Netzah* is *Hod,* the eighth *sefirah,* which means "Splendor". *Hod* symbolizes the left leg of God, representing the material world of sensation, and is often considered to be a lower manifestation of *Gevurah* (Justice). As such, *Hod* gives physical form to *Netzah* and together, the two *sefirot*—much like *Hesed* and *Gevurah*—serve as the channel through which God governs His creation and represent a source of prophecy. While *Netzah* is identified as Moses, *Hod* is associated with Aaron, the older brother of Moses. Thus, the two *sefirot* are regarded as fraternal twins.

9- *Yesod:* Located in the middle of the *Tree of Life,* right between *Netzah* and *Hod,* is the ninth *sefirah, Yesod,* which means "Foundation". Also known as *Yesod Olam,* (Foundation of the World), *Yesod* represents the power of creation or the *"procreative life force of the universe".* It thus acts as a bridge between the upper *sefirot* and the final *sefirah, Malkhut,* channeling the Divine energy and power flowing downwards through the upper triads, to the base of the *Tree,* which represents the physical human world. *Yesod* is also identified as Joseph, the son of Jacob.

10-*Malkhut:* Sitting at the base of the *Tree of Life* is the tenth and final *sefirah, Malkhut,* which means "Kingdom". *Malkhut* symbolizes the feet of God and represents the union between the spiritual and physical worlds. It is through *Malkhut* that the combined energies of all the preceding *sefirot* are transmitted to the physical world. It thus serves as the final receiving *sefirah* on the *Tree of Life,* which provides material form to all other emanations, representing *"God's dominion or power"* on earth. While it is the lowest *sefirah* on the *Tree of Life, Malkhut* is regarded as the highest point of the human world, being described in the *Zohar* as *"the agent for all, from the upper world to the lower world".*

Malkhut is also commonly known as *Shekhinah,* which means "Divine Presence". Often defined as the Divine Feminine, *Shekhinah* is a manifestation of the female or feminine aspect of God and represents His dwelling place or "presence" in the physical world. Sitting at the apex of the human world, *Shekhinah* symbolizes the mother of the lower world, just as *Binah* represents the mother of the upper world. As such, all of creation is regarded as *"the work of Shekhinah"*, who preserves and sustains it *"as a mother cares for her children"*. *Shekhinah* is also described as the daughter of *Hokhmah* and *Binah* and perceived as the "Bride" of *Tiferet*, who represents her "Bridegroom". At the same time, unlike the balanced and perpetual union between *Hokhmah* and *Binah*, *Shekhinah* is separated from *Tiferet* by the sins of the Israelites and has thus fallen into exile along with them.

Shekhinah is described by Kabbalists as *"a part of God"* that is exiled from Himself. The *Zohar* beautifully expresses this separation by alluding it to *"a man who was in love with a woman who lived in the street of the tanners. If she had not been there, he would never have set foot in the place"*. This separation thus symbolizes God's devotion to His Beloved, *Shekhinah*, whose dwelling amidst the exiled children of Israel marked His promise to never forsake them and their land, by always being connected to them through *Shekhinah*.

Shekhinah's separation from *Tiferet* is also traced back to the original sin of Adam, which caused all the channels between heaven and earth to be broken, as *Shekhinah* *"withdrew* and the bond was severed", leading to a cosmic imbalance. *Shekhinah* thus longs to be reunited with her Beloved by restoring the Divine balance.

According to the *Zohar*, this imbalance is rooted in the sins of those that reside in the *"lower world"*, who due to their lack of virtue and faith, have suppressed the *"light"* of *Shekhinah*, causing her to become *"closed up"*, as it is stated:

"When the righteous increase in the world, then the land [Shekhinah] produces fruit and is filled with everything. But when the wicked increase in the world, then it is written: "The waters disappear from the sea".
—The *Zohar*

It is thus through the collective faith of the people that their bond with the Divine Mother, *Shekhinah*, can heal and nourish, so she may one more be reunited with her Beloved through the *"unification of the Holy One"*, thereby restoring the Divine balance.

The Divine union between *Shekhinah* and *Tiferet* is also believed to be cultivated through the sexual union between the husband and wife through marriage, which is regarded by Kabbalists as a sacred union that serves as a *"symbolic realization of the union of God and Shekhinah"*.

Shekhinah/Malkhut is also identified as David—the second king of the twelve tribes of Israel—and a central figure in Judaism, Christianity, Islam and other religions.

12

The structure of the Tree of Life

Each of the three triads which come together to form the *Tree of Life,* represent a separate and distinct facet of God's Being. As such, the first triad—which is composed of *Keter, Hokhmah* and *Binah*—symbolizes the realm of intellect, representing the Mind of God *"thinking through you and realizing the object of His thought in you"*.

The second triad, which is made up of *Hesed, Gevurah* and *Tiferet,* symbolizes the spiritual realm and represents the moral perfection and power of God. The third triad—which comprises *Netzah, Hod* and *Yesod*—on the other hand, symbolizes the realm of nature and reflects the Divine guidance and providence over the world, while the tenth *sefirah, Malkhut/Shekhinah,* symbolizes the physical realm.

Apart from the triads, another common way Kabbalists arrange the *sefirot* on the *Tree of Life* is by dividing them into three vertical columns: the right column, the left column and the central column.

The right column, which is composed of *Hokhmah, Hesed* and *Netzah,* is known as "the Pillar of Mercy" and is represented by the Hebrew letter *"Shin".* The *sefirot* located in this column possess a masculine aspect and are associated with the element of fire.

The left column consists of *Binah, Gevurah* and *Hod* and is titled "the Pillar of Judgment" or "the Pillar of Severity". This column is represented by the Hebrew letter *"Mem"* and associated with the element of water. The *sefirot* that lie within the left column alternatively possess a feminine aspect.

The central column is made up of *Keter,* which sits at the top; *Tiferet,* which is located at the center; and *Yesod* and *Malkhut,* which rest at the bottom. This column is known as "the Pillar of Compassion" or "the Pillar of Mildness" and is represented by the Hebrew letter *"Aleph".* This column is associated with the element of air and symbolizes *"the breath".*

As such, the right and left columns represent opposite and conflicting forces, whereby the right column (the Pillar of Mercy) manifests growth and expansion, while the left column (the Pillar of Severity) manifests contraction and restraint. Much like the

Taoist concept of the *yin* and *yang,* these forces—despite their conflicting nature—are complementary to one another, being thus balanced by the central Pillar of Compassion which unifies Mercy with Severity and Judgment, and establishes and maintains order in the universe.

13

Daat: The hidden knowledge

While the Kabbalists essentially identify ten *sefirot* forming the *Tree of Life,* there is a secret attribute concealed within it, known as *Daat,* meaning "Knowledge". Though *Daat* is not generally recognized by Kabbalists as a separate *sefirah,* it is regarded as a hidden component of the *Tree of Life* that is not necessarily depicted in every representation of the *Tree of Life*—thus symbolizing its concealment marked by its empty space. Situated on the central column of the *Tree, Daat* sits between *Keter* (Crown) and *Tiferet* (Beauty) and represents Divine knowledge, embodying the union of all ten *sefirot* as one, within a single *sefirah.* As such, *Daat* is often perceived as the external image of the *sefirah, Keter,* and reflects the unification of *Hokhmah* (Wisdom) and *Binah* (Understanding). It is also believed by certain traditions to symbolize the face or throat of God.

In *Lurianic* Kabbalah, the *sefirah, Keter,* is omitted in the *Tree of Life* and in fact replaced with *Daat,* which represents the conscious and "known" form of the unconscious *Keter. Daat* is also believed to be associated with miracles tracing back to disciples of Isaac Luria, who were able to *"fly through the air"* by channeling its sacred light.

14

The Four Worlds

In keeping with the concept of the *Ein Sof* (the Divine Infinite) and the ten *sefirot,* Kabbalistic thought explains the relationship between God and Creation through a profound exploration of spiritual realms. The idea of the Four Worlds is therefore central to Jewish mysticism, particularly *Lurianic* Kabbalah, which describes the process of Creation through a descending chain of existence called *"seder hishtalshelus"* (The Order of Development)—similar to the Neoplatonic *chain of being.*

Since all of Creation is believed to be composed of Four primary Realms, the chain of existence is explained specifically with reference to *"tzimtzum"* which means *"withdrawal or retraction of Divine consciousness that precedes Creation".* Tzimtzum is often likened to the Primordial Man, *Adam Kadmon,* who metaphorically (and sometimes literally) depicts the state of the Divine Infinite prior to self-manifestation. As such, the inclusion of the Primordial

Man in the *chain of being* results in the Five Worlds, wherein God is believed to have initiated the process of Creation by contracting His infinite Light to allow a void or space (*"Tehiru"*) for the existence of finite realms.

Based largely on the teachings of the Holy *Ari*, belief in the Four (or Five) Worlds forms the cornerstone of *Lurianic* Kabbalah. In contemporary interpretations, the definition of *tzimtzum* is simply broken down into *"condensations of Ohr (Divine Light)"* to explain the process of Creation. In doing so, it touches upon the law of duality to justify God's presence as well as absence in the spiritual realms.

Despite their distinctions, however, the Four Worlds are believed to be inseparable by virtue of a Divine paradox which essentially unites them. This is a deep reflection on the very nature of existence, whereby the *"descending chain"* illustrates the relative distance between God and His Creation. To that end, the ten *sefirot* suffuse each of the Four Worlds, thus determining their closeness to the Ultimate Source.

The Worlds that exist in close proximity to the *Ein Sof* are deemed 'Higher Realms' and the relatively distant are known to be 'Lesser Realms'. The Divine Light, however, permeates each of these Worlds— although it is considerably diluted upon descending into Lesser Realms which denote lower levels of consciousness. The emanation of Divine Light is mentioned in the Book of Isaiah in the following words:

*"Every one that is called by My name And for
My glory (Atziluth "Emanation"),
I have created (Ber'iah "Creation"),
I have formed (Yetzirah "Formation"),
even I have made (Asiyah "Action")."*

—Isaiah (43:7)

Understanding the Four Worlds is crucial to the discipline of Kabbalah as it delves into the distinctions between creation, formation and action, thus serving as an exemplary model for spiritual ascension or human experience. The primordial fifth world is often excluded from the list for it more or less illustrates God as the Archetypal Man, transcending form altogether. Moreover, it is represented by *Keter* (Crown), which is the Divine will (for creation)—elevated above the remaining *sefirot* in the *Tree of Life*. Since all ideas of creation exist only in potential within this Realm, it is therefore superior to the Four Worlds.

1. *Atziluth* (The World of 'Emanation'): Derived from the Hebrew word *"Aitzel"* which means "emanated from", *Atziluth* is the Highest of the Four Worlds because it is still contained within the realm of the Infinite. Without an independent state of existence, therefore, *Atziluth* is the purest manifestation of Divinity for, unlike other Realms, it is united wholly with its source—a concept notably depicted through the *Tree of Life*. Consequently, the World of Emanation represents the ten *sefirot*, with *Hokhma* (Wisdom) being the most dominant, wherein all creations go beyond the polarity of 'good' and 'bad'. Within this World, souls and Divine emanations are unaware of their existence since they are not separate from the *Ein Sof*.

2. *Ber'iah* (The World of 'Creation'): This Realm is usually described in conjunction with the Latin phrase *"creatio ex nihilo"* which means *"creation out of Nothingness"*. Often referred to as "The Higher Garden of Eden" (where the highest ranking Angels reside) or "The Divine Throne", *Ber'iah* is where the Divine Infinite first descends in order to pass through to the lower worlds. In this Realm, existence is not confined to shape or form, though unlike *Atziluth*, the creations of *Ber'iah* are very much aware that they exist. Additionally, the World of Creation is ruled by the second intellectual *sefirah* known as *Binah* (Understanding), which is fundamentally feminine in nature.

The Higher Garden of Eden is also tied closely to the story of Ezekiel—narrated in the Torah—which gives us a glimpse into a dimension far beyond the physical world. It is, in fact, Ezekiel's account of the winged creatures (of *Ber'iah*) which ultimately led to the introduction of *Merkabah* (chariot mysticism) in practical Kabbalah. The account is relayed in the *Tanakh* (Hebrew Bible) in the following words:

"Now it came to pass in the thirtieth year in the fourth [month] on the fifth day of the month, as I was in the midst of the exile by the river Chebar—the heavens opened up, and I saw visions of God. [...] And I saw, and behold, a tempest was coming from the north, a huge cloud and a flaming fire with a brightness around it; and from its midst, it was like the color of the chashmal from the midst of the fire. [...]And from its midst was the likeness of four living beings [...]And I saw the living beings, and behold, one wheel [was] on the ground beside the living beings for its four faces. The appearance of the wheels and their work was like the appearance of crystal, and the four of them had one likeness, and their appearance and their workings were as a wheel would be within a wheel."

—Ezekiel (1:16)

3. *Yetzirah* (The World of 'Formation'):
Third of the four celestial worlds in the *Tree
of Life, Yetzirah* is also known as "The Lower
Garden of Eden"—a world defined by general
existence, as opposed to formless existence in
the former Realm. The distinction between
"creation" and "formation" is of great
cosmological significance in Kabbalah,
especially when discussing the *chain of being*.

This is to lay emphasis on the Order of
Development which expounds on the process
of Creation by differentiating between the
four stages. While matter is essentially
created in *Ber'iah, Yetzirah* is where that
matter is fashioned into basic elements
through finite plans. Dominating this Realm
are six emotional *sefirot,* from *Chesed*
(Loving-kindness) to *Yesod* (Foundation).
These attributes are chiefly associated with
the main angels of *Yetzirah* who, upon
recognizing their separation from the Divinity
of *Atziluth,* burn with ecstatic longing for
consummation.

4. *Asiyah* (The World of 'Action'): This is the world of particular existence, where matter is deemed 'complete' owing primarily to the concealment of the Divine Infinite. Lower angels play an active role in spiritual *Asiyah*, where the most dominant *sefirah* is *Malkhut* (Fulfillment in Kingship).

The last two *sefirot* in spiritual *Asiyah* channel the lifeforce in the lowest Realm of existence just below it, known as *Asiyah Gashmi* (Physical *Asiyah*). Within this World, existence is purely physical in nature and creation is molded into material form, visible to the naked eye. It is here that our Universe actually begins—due, in large part, to the severe dilution of Divine energy which finally allows for a purely tangible existence.

While the Four Worlds are massively different in their design and purpose, they are ultimately connected and unified by the Divine lifeforce which flows through them—even if it is weakened in descent due to the presence of material elements. In *Hasidic* philosophy, the Four Worlds capture the perfect unity of Creation, reflecting Divine immanence within and beyond the earthly plane of existence. In addition, these Realms also denote the four levels of human consciousness in ascending order, with *Asiyah* representing Action; *Yetzirah,* Emotion; *Ber'iah,* Intellect; and *Atziluth,* the Spirit/Soul. In spiritual ascension, the soul must transition between the four stages in order to find union with the *Ein Sof*—a process which takes place in the Highest state of consciousness when the soul can finally see beyond the limitations of the physical world.

15

Qliphoth and the necessity of Evil

One of the most fascinating aspects of Kabbalah is discovering how duality forms the basis of all Creation—ultimately revealing the Divine paradox as a fundamental belief, crucial to the realization of Divine Reality. As we explore the attributes of the *Ein Sof,* taking into account the notion of *tzimtzum,* we are bound to identify a strong correlation between duality and Divine manifestation that is of particular significance in Jewish mysticism.

Retrospectively, for the existence of the *Tree of Life,* there exists also an inverted *Tree of Life* (the *Qliphothic* Tree of Death) with ten adverse *sefirot*—alternatively referred to as 'The Order of Demons'. When delving into the origins of Creation, therefore, it is imperative that we study as well the nature of evil, so we may understand how it is woven into the fabric of existence in a world that is essentially created and sustained by an omnibenevolent God.

In Kabbalah, evil is represented through, what is known as, *"qliphoth"* (husks/shells)—immediately adding dimension to the otherwise generic definition of the term, generally reduced to the absence of 'good'. It is worth considering that the metaphor is, first and foremost, effective in adding purpose to the concept of evil, seeing as both "husks" and "shells" refer to a protective shield that guards a potentially valuable and defenseless object. Furthermore, in light of this metaphor, the purpose served is a seemingly positive one—that of protection and endurance—in turn, suggesting the necessity of evil rather than a conquest.

This portrayal of evil takes after the Kabbalistic belief in *Satia A'hra* (The Other Side)—a polar reflection of the Holy Realm, created within the vacuum of *tzimtzum*. For all intents and purposes, The Other Side exists as the opposing manifestation of Divine Reality—the Anti-World where everything is essentially created from anti-matter. As a parallel to the Holy Realm, The Other Side puts into question the very nature of evil, along with its exclusive attribution to Satan. Conversely, rabbinic literature interprets *Satia A'hra* as a direct manifestation of God Himself, much like the Holy Realm—which propels criticism from those who see evil as a separation from, and not a part of, the Divine Infinite.

Through this postulation, Kabbalah draws our attention to an endemic flaw within Creation called *"Shevirah"*, which is the shattering of the vessel (for the existence of a more orderly world). This is in reference to the shattering of *"Tohu"*—the World of Chaos—where the originally emanated *sefirot* were too intense in nature to form a stable Universe. It is believed that *Tehiru* (the primordial void or space) could not contain emanations of Divine Light, consequently shattering the vessel and transforming the ten *sefirot* into reconfigured emanations called *Partzufim* (Divine Faces) which thus came to define the Four Worlds.

In addition, *Shevirah* led to the scattering of "Divine sparks" in the material realm, where they remain trapped and await redemption to this day. The phrase "order out of chaos" is originally based on *Shevirah,* which highlights the contrast between *Tohu* (the World of Chaos) and *Tikkun* (the World of Order), forming the basis of duality in the process of creation.

Divine sparks are contained within the *qliphoth* to keep them from dissipating entirely for they are essentially 'pieces of God', held in 'exile' for the purpose of creation. Without the demonic Realm, therefore, the Divine sparks would disperse— ultimately finding union with the Divine source—and undo the existence of finite realms altogether. It is through the impurity of human sin that the shells are thickened and the *qliphoth,* strengthened, consequently maintaining a cosmic balance which perpetuates the separation between God and Creation.

Similarly, the purity of good deeds weaken the shell, allowing Divine sparks to break free from confinement and merge with the Divine Infinite—an act of *"tikkun olam"*, which is humanity's collective responsibility to repair and thus heal the world. Kabbalists build on this belief by connecting it to the role of humanity, suggesting that every human being contains the Divine spark—that it is up to each of us to bring forth the Messianic Age by overcoming the illusions of this temporary realm and finding our way back to the Divine Source. When the world is besieged by violence and catastrophe, *tikkun olam* is delayed and the process of redemption, lengthened.

As such, evil works as a proactive tool which sustains the existence of Creation. Adding to this belief, Kabbalists argue that just as the ten *sefirot* represent the attributes of God, *Satia A'hra* too sheds light on the nature of Divine Order. Accordingly, evil is believed to be contributing to the Divine law rather than destroying it—for without The Other Side, the Holy Realm would cease to exist.

Between the dichotomy of 'good' and 'evil', there exists the power of free will which Man exercises through Divine Judgment—represented by the fifth *sefirah*, *"Gevurah"* (Strength/Judgment/Severity). The root of evil stems primarily from the imbalance of this *sefirah* and if decisions are made on the basis of faulty judgment, chaos ensues in the natural world thereby making real the illusory world of Evil.

Kabbalists interpret evil as a necessity that essentially allows the exercising of free will. It is because of existing between the *Ein Sof* and The Holy Realm that evil naturally compels human beings to act upon choice. In essence, human sin would not be truly demonic were it not committed in the spirit of free will—that is to say, Evil would not be 'evil' without the choice to do 'good' and vice versa.

16

Levels of the Soul

Since all human beings contain the Holy Light of the *Ein Sof,* Kabbalah pays close attention to the spiritual dimension of human existence in order to understand our intricate connection with the Divine. Accordingly, it expounds on five levels of the human Soul which are linked to the Five parallel Realms existing beyond the physical plane. The last three levels of the Soul, however, are subject to greater scrutiny since the remaining Realms denote higher levels of consciousness and thus exceed our knowledge and understanding. In ascending order, the five levels of the Soul are *Nefesh* (linked to *Asiyah*), *Ru'ach* (linked to *Yetzirah*), *Nashamah* (linked to *Ber'iah*), *Chayah* (linked to *Atziluth*) and *Ye'hida* (linked to *Adam Kadmon*).

Nefesh: This is the lowest level of the Soul, made manifest at the time of physical birth. As a result, it is closely tied to instinct and physical activity, both of which correspond with the 'animal spirit'. *Nefesh* does not leave the body immediately after death, and instead waits until it is completely decomposed—highlighting its attachment to the vessel and the reason why it is linked to the lowest realm of existence. The *sefirah* of Action rules this level of consciousness, suggesting the Divine service of acknowledging (and submitting to) the Divine Infinite. Within this stage lies the greatest concealment of Divinity, therefore, if the Soul can realize and submit to the idea of the *Ein Sof*, it can easily tap into higher consciousness.

Ru'ach: Referred to as the fourth level of the *Soul*, *Ru'ach* connects *Nefesh* to *Nashamah*. It manifests in the form of emotions—allowing the development of personal traits—and corresponds to the angels of *Yetzirah*. When the Soul reaches this level of consciousness, it is driven by the *sefirah* of Intellect which entails Divine service through contemplation. This is to amplify the emotions of love and awe, so they can be directed towards God for cosmic rectification. Since this is a relatively low level of consciousness, however, the love felt for God is still limited because it contemplates lower levels of Divine energy.

Nashamah: At this stage, the Soul contemplates the manifestation of Divine energy, revealing its ties to the World of *Ber'iah* (World of Creation). Since the *sefirah* of Understanding is predominant in this consciousness, the Soul can finally reflect on *"creation out of Nothingness"*. This is when the one-dimensional, ephemeral aspects of God are dismissed in light of His eternal attributes. One of the major signs of having reached this stage is experiencing *"rapture of the heart"* when pondering over the subject of the Divine. The spontaneity of Love indicates communion with God, marking a sharp contrast with the reaction felt in *Ru'ach*.

Chayah: Considered to be the second highest state of consciousness, *Chayah* represents complete nullification of the ego. It is in this state that the Soul stops associating God with finite Realms, and begins identifying Him with "Non-being"—One who exceeds the limitations of conceivable thought. While *Ru'ach* revolves around *"creation out of Nothingness"*, *Chayah* is centered on diminishing of the self to pave the way for a renewed identity. This is when the Soul shatters self-image in the temporary world by existing wholly in the Divine Infinite. The purity of Love felt for God ultimately leads to knowledge of the Absolute Truth, which makes this level considerably superior to *Nashamah*.

Ye'hida: Following *Chayah, Ye'hida* represents the highest possible state of Divine consciousness. This is when the Soul reflects the Holy Light by being eternally bound to the transcendent *Adam Kadmon*—having fully merged with God. Very few are able to make it this far in the chain of spiritual evolution, and those who succeed, do so at the expense of martyrdom or self-sacrifice in the service of God or all of humanity.

17

Reincarnation

Although the concept of reincarnation is not specifically discussed in traditional Kabbalah (the *Tanakh* and early rabbinic literature), it is nevertheless famously advocated by followers of the Holy *Ari* who, along with other renowned Kabbalist teachers, count it among the key pillars of Jewish mysticism. Described as *"the transmigration of souls"*, reincarnation is explained in accordance with the aforementioned *tikkun olam*—that is, humanity's collective responsibility to repair the world.

In *Lurianic* Kabbalah, it is given the name *"Gilgul"* and is fundamentally in keeping with the idea of spiritual ascension. Since human beings contain the Divine spark, they must take it upon themselves to aid in cosmic rectification by reaching the highest level of Divine consciousness. This is where *gilgul* comes into play, asserting the need to accomplish the Divine task of spiritual reparation (*Tikun*). If the Soul is unable to do this in one lifetime, it will be reincarnated in a different vessel to finish the job—such is the necessity of cosmic redemption.

According to this perspective, *gilgul* is the realization that the Soul must feel whole again by returning to the Divine Source from whence it came, which can only be made possible by undoing the damage caused by previous actions (echoing the Original Sin). There is, however, a limit to the number of times the Soul is given a chance to redeem itself. If it undertakes the process of *Tikun* in three consecutive lifetimes, it is reincarnated as many times as it takes thereafter to find communion with the *Ein Sof.* Alternatively, if it indulges in wrongdoing, deviating from the Divine path in three consecutive lifetimes, the cycle of reincarnation ends and the Soul is presumably destroyed.

There are many ways to achieve spiritual reparation, one of which is the observance of the 613 *"Mitzvot"* (Judaic commandments). The number 613 is held in high regard, considered to be an ancient esoteric code illustrating the Divine Order—there are 613 veins in the human body, along with 613 bones—each corresponding to the 613 parts of the Soul. Each of these parts must be repaired through the *Mitzvot* until it can ascend to a higher level, ultimately reaching *Ye'hida.*

18

Primary texts

All Kabbalistic texts are ultimately based on the "Oral Torah", whose esoteric teachings were once deemed potentially dangerous if exposed to the common man. Although the Torah was originally delivered to Moses in the form of written scrolls, it took all of 40 days to reveal the Divine secrets contained therein. As such, the Word of God was passed down orally to generations for 1,400 years out of adherence to the Divine Law—hence the name "Oral Torah" to distinguish from the written Torah. Concurrently, it is also suggested that the roots of the Torah can be traced back to Abraham, who discovered the laws of Nature by observing his inner self—which, in turn, reflects the underlying principles of Kabbalah.

In order to protect the teachings of the Oral Torah, teachers would often impart their knowledge to one disciple at a time, prohibiting the use of written word to explain the mysteries of the Unknown. Similar attempts were made to keep the tradition alive and thus this sacred wisdom was revealed only to a select group of people who were entrusted to maintain the code of secrecy. It was not until after the destruction of the Second Temple of Jerusalem in 70 CE that the teachings were written down in order to preserve the law.

Accordingly, the first redaction of the Oral Torah—called the *"Mishnah"* ("Repetition")—was written in 200 CE by Rabbi Yahudah Hannasi, who is accredited for laying the foundations of rabbinic literature. In 500 CE, it underwent further revisions by prominent rabbis of The Land of Israel and Babylonia, who included within it their commentary and analysis of the text, also known as the *"Gemara"* ("to study").

Together, the *Mishnah* and the *Gemara* gave birth to the *Talmud* which marks the beginning of the spread of Kabbalah. Stretching up to 6,200 pages in length, it forms the central tenets of Kabbalah, including the *Halakha* (Jewish law), ethics, history and philosophy. The oldest surviving manuscript of the *Talmud* is the *Munich Talmud* from the year 1342.

Arguably the most important Kabbalistic text after the *Talmud* is the *"Zohar"* ("The Book of Splendor")—widely acknowledged as a major influence on the entire discipline of Jewish mysticism. It is usually associated with the writings of Rabbi Simoen bar Yochai, but also attributed to Rabbi Moses de Leon, who claimed to have discovered it in Spain in the 13th century. The book deals primarily with mysticism and mythical cosmogony, alternatively viewed as an esoteric interpretation of rabbinic literature called *Midrash*.

Aside from foundational texts, one of the primary sources for Kabbalah is the *Sefer Yetzirah* ("The Book of Formation") which delves into mathematical and linguistic analyses of the cosmos. The historical origins of the book are highly debated—with some sources attributing it to the 6th CE, while others speculate it was written by Abraham and edited by Akiva ben Joseph (described in the *Talmud* as *"Head of the Sages"*). Renowned German philologist and Gnostic scholar, August Reitzenstein, claimed that the origins of the *Sefer Yetzirah* could be as old as 2nd century CE, though it is also believed by some to be a much older text, passed on from Adam to Abraham to Noah and so forth.

Among other writings is the pseudo-epigraphical *"Haichalot"* ("Heavenly Palaces"), commonly believed to be from the post-rabbinical era. While the exact date and authorship of *Haichalot* is unknown, the content provides deep insight into the journey of spiritual ascension through the heavenly realms—an essential underpinning of *Merkabah* (chariot mysticism in Kabbalah). The book does not contain a singular fluid text; rather it is a collection of esoteric writings which shed light on various accounts of heavenly ascent, including Rabbi Ishmael's visit to the Seventh Heaven, called *"Haichalot Rabbati"*.

A similar epigraphical text which influenced Kabbalistic thought, albeit more notably, was the *Bahir* ("Book of Illumination"), commonly attributed to Rabbi Nehunya ben Hakana who wrote it in the 1st century CE—though medieval and modern Kabbalists argue over the authenticity of this claim. Despite 12,000 words in length, the book is considered an important Kabbalistic doctrine which draws upon the mystical significance of the Hebrew alphabet as well as the *Sefer Yetzirah.* In addition, it explains the use of sacred names in *magick,* all of which is almost entirely written in the form of a dialogue between a master and disciple.

Having gained recognition in wider circles, the *"Sefer Raziel Hemalakh"* ("The Book of Raziel the Angel") is another book worth mentioning—a practical Kabbalah *grimoire* (textbook on the subject of ancient magic). As with most Kabbalistic texts, the origins of the book are obscure, though it is unanimously agreed that much of its content dates back to the 13th century, owing to a surviving manuscript written by Alfonso X, the King of Castile, León and Galicia. Since it is a compilation of different writings, however, certain sections of the book indicate a much older periodization.

Historians also argue over the authorship of *Sefer Raziel Hemalakh,* however, a large part is generally attributed to the Chessidei Ashkenaz (Jewish mystics of the 12th and 13th century). It is also suggested that the book was delivered to Adam by the Angel Raziel, who then passed it to Noah and King Solomon. The book essentially explores the laws of Nature with reference to *gematria* (sacred geometry), astrology, angelology and alchemy. Due to elaborate details concerning ancient spells, invocations, guidelines to creating and wearing amulets and talismans—among other things—The Book of Raziel gained notoriety in Europe, particularly for its focus on rites and rituals that allegedly opened the doors to necromancy.

The more recent works in Kabbalah are dated back to the 16th century, one of which is *"Pardes Rimonim"* ("Pardes, Orchard of Pomegranates"). Written by renowned Jewish mystic, Moses ben Jacob Cordovero, the book offers a unique interpretation of the *Zohar*—a school of thought that subsequently led to the inception of Cordoverian Kabbalah.

In the same century, the teachings of Rabbi Isaac Luria were published in Safed by his disciple, Haim Vital, as a book titled *"Etz Hayim"* ("The *Tree of Life"*)—laying the groundwork for what was to be *Lurianic* Kabbalah. In later years, Haim Vital's son, Shmuel Vital, published the remaining works of his father under the title *"Shemona She'arim"* ("The Eight Gates"). It provides a more comprehensive analysis and explanation of *Lurianic* Kabbalah, since the Holy *Ari* never recorded any of his own teachings in written form.

Oracle Claretta Pam

19

Customs and Practices

The more experiential aspects of Jewish mysticism can be found in its customs and practices which are based largely on meditation and prayer. Despite notable distinctions between Theoretical, Meditative and Practical Kabbalah, following rituals is common to all three schools of thought—even though the nature of these rituals may vary considerably. Unlike Practical Kabbalah, however, common practices in Theoretical and Meditative Kabbalah mostly include traditional Jewish ones, such as the Torah study and observance of the 613 *Mitzvot* (Judaic commandments). As such, the difference between orthodox Jewish practices and Kabbalistic ones lie in the *kavanah* (proper intention) upon which the *Mitzvot* take effect.

In most cases, traditional Jewish festivals and holidays such as the *Shabbat* ("Sabbath"), *Hannukah* ("Festival of Lights") and *Yom Kippur* ("Day of Atonement") are seen by Kabbalists as opportunities for a unique mystical experience wherein each practice—no matter how small—contributes to one's understanding of God and helps to reach a higher level of Divine consciousness. Certain types of meditation, however, are exclusive to Kabbalah, and not necessarily practiced by orthodox Jews. It is worth mentioning that Practical Kabbalah encourages an entirely different set of rituals which incorporate ancient *magick* and occult practices that are strictly prohibited by Theoretical and Meditative traditions.

20

Mystical Exegesis

While reading and reciting the Torah is a fundamentally Jewish practice, Kabbalists are widely known for identifying mathematical and linguistic secrets encoded within the text in an attempt to uncover hidden mystical truths. Ancient manuscripts such as the Torah, the *Talmud,* the *Zohar* and certain works of rabbinic literature are laced with esoteric symbols and allegories, and thus studied in Kabbalah with the purpose of unraveling some of the greatest mysteries of this world and beyond. Along with Jewish writings, text from other scriptures—such as the Bible—are also studied closely in order to gain insight into spiritual laws and draw connections between Divine revelations.

Much of the decoding involves the use of *Gematria* (sacred geometry) to find concealed messages, such as the hidden names of God in Hebrew letters which are said to contain immense power and energy. Secrets decoded from within the text are then used in meditation and prayer, drawing on the power of the sacred names for a spiritually enriching experience that is otherwise difficult to create (due to the impurity of human thought and actions). Alternatively, in Practical Kabbalah, the sacred names are used in occult practices and incantations to increase the potency of *magick* rituals. This is why mystical exegeses are conducted in secrecy, so as to prevent the abuse of Divine   secrets.

21

Prayer

Invoking the sacred names of God is particularly important in Kabbalistic prayer, wherein the prayer denotes the union between the Individual with the Divine Infinite through *Kavanah* ("mystical intentions")—ultimately triggering spiritual ascent. This forms the very basis of Meditative Kabbalah, which draws upon the idea of using the Holy names of God to raise Divine consciousness. Such forms of prayer can be traced back to the religious practices of Abraham, Isaac and Jacob, who encouraged praying thrice a day—once in the morning, followed by once in the afternoon and finally once in the evening.

In most cases, a standard Kabbalistic prayer is offered with the ultimate aim to destroy the Self in order to make room for the Light (of God). As such, calling upon God by His infinite names is a means to nullify the ego—without which, the prayer is essentially void of depth and meaning, thus convoluting its purpose entirely. In the given context, the goal of the *Kavanah* is to redirect and focus one's consciousness on specific *sefirot* by reciting words that correspond to them directly. This is in keeping with the idea of spiritual ascension, whereby prayer is an attempt to elevate the Soul to the highest stage so it can experience communion with the Divine. Through this procedure, Kabbalists infuse the basic premise of *Merkabah* mysticism into conventional Jewish prayer service, thereby following the orthodox tradition of staying connected with the community as well as catering to the individual needs of the Soul, all at the same time.

This method of offering prayer was made famous by Rabbi Isaac Luria sometime in the 16th century—particularly his interpretation of prayer as an experiential, transformative process as opposed to a repetitive exercise grounded on empty speech and insufficient concentration. Additionally, it was also the Holy *Ari* who developed the tradition of praying using specific *kevanot* for the different names of God. This practice was followed by the discovery of spiritual depth and vibrancy underlying Hebrew words and their numerical codes—a prime example being the *Tetragrammaton*.

According to the founder of *Hasidism*, Rabbi Yisroel bin Eliezer, prayer is a powerful tool wherein every word in the prayer is a way to align oneself with a corresponding Realm beyond the physical world. In light of this belief, unification in the Divine Realms is made possible through the recitation of sacred Hebrew words—a prayer described by *Ba'al Shem Tov* as *"a world within itself"*. The most powerful words are believed to be those that send praise to God—for they transport the Soul to transcendental states of awareness—ultimately leading to the realization of Divine immanence. In essence, words that are uttered in praise of God enable the individual to dissolve all material and social desires for the sole purpose of experiencing Divine union.

While there are many different kinds of prayer services in Kabbalah, *Shema Yisrael* ("listen/hear/understand") is considered to be the most important among orthodox Jews and Kabbalists, alike. Based on the pillars of monotheistic Judaism, the prayer allows unification in the Upper Realms through acknowledging the unity of God with perfect *kavanah*. It is narrated in the *Tanakh* (Hebrew Bible) in the following words:

"Hear, O Israel: the Lord our God, the Lord is one. And thou shalt love the Lord thy God with all thy heart, and with all thy soul, and with all thy might."

—Deuteronomy (6:4-5)

In Kabbalah, to practice the *Shema* is to bear witness to the Divine Unity of the Higher and Lower worlds which encapsulate the Oneness of God. Since the *Tetragrammaton* ("YHVH") is difficult to express in the English language, it is thus described in the Zohar as a unique expression of Divine Union between the *Tiferet* and *Shekhinah*—crucial to the spiritual reparation of our physical world.

22

Meditation

In almost every system of belief, prayer is commonly supplemented with meditation because of the predominance of spirituality in religious practices. Similarly, Kabbalah portrays meditation as an ancient form of contemplation that seeks to align the Soul with the Higher Realms in an attempt to reunite with the Divine Source. This is mostly achieved in trance-induced meditations that are centered on achieving closeness to the Divine Infinite—also referred to as *"Deveikut"* ("cleaving to God").

Due to inaccuracy in the translations of Hebrew writings, however, many ancient forms of meditations are either erroneously complicated or altogether incomprehensible. To take an example, the very word for meditation in Hebrew—*"Hitbodedut"*—is often subject to confusion as it translates into "self-isolation" which can have a number of interpretations. While some take it to mean physical isolation, Kabbalists understand it to mean mental isolation, in keeping with the ideas of Haim Vital—a renowned disciple of the Holy *Ari*. It is through this interpretation of "self-isolation" that Kabbalists explore the concept of meditation—which is essentially the need to isolate the Soul from the body to reach a certain state of enlightenment.

The importance of self-isolation is reiterated in all Kabbalistic meditations, for the Soul must first realize that it does not belong to the physical world if it is to return to the Divine Infinite. Through detachment from the physical world, one can go beyond the limitations of perceptive faculties and thus shatter all illusions of identity reinforced in the lowest realm of existence. By secluding oneself from one's thoughts, therefore, the Soul enters into a state of isolation where it no longer identifies with its physical body.

This is no easy realization to attain, however, as those who walk the spiritual path often forewarn. While it is relatively easy to attain physical isolation— by cutting away all ties with the community—isolating the Soul from its physical body is a process that may take much longer. This is where the contrast between physical and mental isolation surfaces, with the former interpreted along the lines of a physical "hideout", and the latter, an attempt to liberate the Soul from the confines of imagination and thought.

Due to the similarities between *"Hitbonenut"* ("contemplation") and *"Hitbodedut"* ("meditation"), the words are often used interchangeably to express common ideas. It is important to keep in mind, however, that although contemplation plays an active role in Kabbalistic meditation, it does not offer a holistic representation of the phenomenon itself. At most, it is a technique commonly employed in meditative practice, but to replace it for "self-isolation" is to fundamentally reduce the essence of Kabbalistic meditation to contemplation alone.

There are three primary distinctions in all Kabbalistic meditations—each one based on three elemental means to achieve *dekeivut*—the intellect, emotions and body. Accordingly, the three means indicate particular styles of meditation that are exclusive to different Kabbalistic traditions. In some cases, however, intellect and emotions are used simultaneously in meditative practice, so as to merge the teachings of Theoretical and Meditative Kabbalah for a more harmonious experience. The different types of meditation are usually described in relation to externally or internally-directed exercises.

Driven by the intellect, externally-focused meditation generally makes use of visualization techniques and contemplative practice. This can be accomplished by focusing on an external object—such as a physical picture—coupled with the utterance of divine names. In *Lurianic* Kabbalah, externally-directed meditation is referred to as *"Yechudim"* ("Unifications") wherein a mental image, rather than a physical one, is contemplated using a combination of predetermined divine names.

In some cases, it is also common to contemplate sacred texts such as the Torah, and delve into the mystical aspects of the commandments to gain a better understanding of the Higher Realms. Similar to this practice is the study of devotional texts for self-improvement. By contemplating the sacred wisdom of Divine law, one can actively pursue cosmic rectification, concurrently elevating the Soul to higher states of enlightenment.

Internally-directed meditation can be practiced using spontaneous thoughts or mental images. It is practiced by focusing on a vague memory or idea, allowing the emergence of random thoughts and images that naturally correspond to it. Due to the nature of this meditation, it is considered largely unstructured compared to other methods. In contrast, emotionally-driven meditation is usually practiced by directing emotional energy and feelings into verbalized words. It is fueled primarily by *kavanah*, which serves as an effective tool to harmonize the Soul with corresponding *sefirot*.

It is also common to integrate music into meditation in order to reach heightened levels of Divine consciousness. The energy associated with musical vibrations, in turn, affects the energy of the Soul, causing it to ascend upon spiritual intoxication. Accordingly, the purpose of the *Yechudim* is thus to alter the state of the Higher Worlds—using the power of the *kavanot* to create Unification between the male (*Tiferet*) and female (*Shekhinah*) energy of the cosmos. This is not to be confused with Practical Kabbalah, however, whose practices entail altering the state of physical reality as opposed to altering the reality of spiritual realms for cosmic redemption. As highlighted, much depends on the intention with which a certain type of meditation is practiced.

The most sought-after approach to meditation is the non-directive, which focuses on stillness of the mind and—with enough practice—achieves complete nullification of (internal and external) perception. This ultimately leads to the realization of Absolute Truth, since the Soul is no longer barred by the parameters of time, matter and space. It is mostly explained with reference to the philosophy of Divine Love.

In Kabbalah, the path of Love is commonly attributed to Maimonides, who encouraged the merging of intellect and emotions when contemplating the nature of the Divine. According to his teachings, meditation that is based on a combination of the two subsequently evokes a deep-rooted appreciation for the wonders of Creation. This is followed by a profound understanding of Divine wisdom which manifests in the form of ecstatic passion called *"Cheshk"*.

The euphoria associated with the aforementioned practice can also be experienced in the meditative traditions of Ecstatic Kabbalah. Abraham Abulafia, founder of Prophetic/Ecsctatic Kabbalah, is largely accredited for writing detailed guides to meditation, using sacred Hebrew words and permutations which lead to "ecstatic states" of Divine consciousness.

This is believed to be the highest state of enlightenment—characterized by rapturous joy and elation—whereby the individual finally experiences Divine Union in the physical realm. It is often within this trance-induced state that some mystics meet their physical demise. In light of this tradition, Prophetic Kabbalah incorporates the use of the body to aid in meditative experience, which generally involves concentrated breathing, swaying of the head and similar levels of physicality to enhance the quality of the practice. The *Tabernacle* ("Festival of Succot") is a primary example of the close connection between meditative dance and enlightenment.

23

Kabbalah in the Modern World

The obscurity surrounding the origins of Kabbalistic texts often suggests mystical antiquity that perhaps predates Judaism. In view of this conjecture, the secrets of Kabbalah can be traced back to prophets and sages—as old as Adam and Abraham—who subsequently passed it to later generations in secrecy, from Isaac to Jacob, Noah to David then Solomon and so forth. This is an interesting contrast to Kabbalah in the modern world which is presented as a celebrity-endorsed cult, driven by expensive Kabbalah centers and sold to masses under the guise of New Age philosophy.

Many of the contemporary teachings relayed in Kabbalah Centers are criticized by traditionalists for their deviation from the norm. One of these is to make public the esoteric secrets of Jewish texts (such as the *Zohar* and *Talmud*) that are meant exclusively for the pious or those of pure intent. Traditionally, it is important to maintain the exclusivity of this knowledge due to the potential dangers of being misused for sinister purposes. Without this protective measure, therefore, imparting Divine secrets could inevitably result in destruction and chaos.

Incidentally, the ancient tradition of transmitting sacred knowledge to a select few has been lost since the inception of the Kabbalah Center. Coupled with the support of celebrities the likes of Madonna, Kabbalah Centers have grown particularly famous in recent years. This can perhaps also be attributed to the growing influence of secret societies and occult practices which have little, if anything, to do with Theoretical and Meditative schools in traditional Kabbalah.

24

The Kabbalah Center

The first Kabbalah Center—established in the United States in 1965—was founded by Philip Berg and Rav Yehuda Tzvi Brandwein as "The National Research Institute of Kabbalah". Berg, who was once an orthodox Rabbi, dabbled in the insurance business before embarking on a journey to share the teachings of Kabbalah with the rest of the world. Following the death of Brandwein, the Institute was reestablished by Berg and his wife, years later in New York, as a not-for-profit organization called "The Kabbalah Center". In 1984, The Kabbalah Center opened its headquarters in Los Angeles, California where it continues to operate to this day—attracting members of the elite who mainly consist of Hollywood celebrities.

According to traditional Judaism, Kabbalah as a mystical tradition should not be explored before the individual is well-versed in ancient Hebrew and has a deep understanding of the *Halakha* ("Jewish law"). This is due to the complex nature of its teachings, which could otherwise be horribly misinterpreted or seem incongruent with the fundamentals of Judaism. In light of this warning, males, in particular, are generally advised not to explore Kabbalah until the age of 40—which is considered the pinnacle of maturity and wisdom in rabbinic literature.

In contrast, the Kabbalah Center opens its doors to anyone and everyone—provided that the Center is paid its financial dues. Alternatively, it offers *"practical methods"* to understand the teachings of Kabbalah, without demanding pre-requisites such as fluency in Hebrew or familiarity with ancient Jewish texts.

This has caused substantial backlash from traditional Kabbalists who see it as a perversion, and thus distortion, of Divine knowledge. Nevertheless, the Kabbalah Center claims to make the sacred teachings more accessible to wider audiences by drawing on the similarities of world faiths—namely Christianity, Judaism and Buddhism—all of which function through a universal system of Divine laws. Consequently, it describes itself as a way to gain deeper insight into religion, rather than a replacement for it—which is one of many reasons behind its likeness to New Age ideology.

Despite its claims to spread the message of universality, the Kabbalah Center has been subject to much criticism, particularly due to a number of financial controversies. In 2011, it was under investigation by the IRS and FBI for its involvement with a project called "Raising Malawi". Initiated by Madonna, the project was meant to provide relief funds to the African nation of Malawi, only to be abandoned when it was discovered that millions of dollars for the project were unaccounted for. Following the incident in 2012, it was reported that the Kabbalah Center accepted a donation worth $600,000 from an elderly dementia patient whose financial advisor had close links to the Center.

In addition, the Kabbalah Center is famous for selling expensive merchandise which includes a red string bracelet to ward off the Evil Eye ("*Ayin Hara*") and exclusive spring water with healing properties that can potentially cure cancer. While the use of ritual objects is based on the teachings of Kabbalah itself, orthodox Kabbalists view the selling of merchandise at high rates as a commodification and commercialization of a sacred mystical tradition.

Celebrity endorsement has also played an active role in garnering media attention for the Kabbalah Center. Although some of them have only been temporarily involved with Kabbalah, their brief association has helped the Center gain considerable recognition and influence in elite circles. Celebrities who have been affiliated with the Center for a short period of time (or more) include Madonna, Demi Moore, Britney Spears, Ashton Kutcher, Elizabeth Taylor, Paris Hilton, Roseanne Barr, Mick Jagger,

Lindsay Lohan, Mischa Barton, Nicole Richie, Rosie O'Donnell, Lucy Liu and Naomi Campbell, among several others. Madonna is largely credited for introducing the Kabbalah Center to influential Hollywood figures. It is, however, common for celebrities to leave the Center for personal reasons— such as Britney Spears who left in 2005—or Jerry Hall, who left in 2006 due to the Center's pressure to tithe ten percent of her revenues.

25

Conclusion

Despite the mystery and esotericism associated with Kabbalah, it may come as a surprise that this ancient tradition holds much in common with the mystical dimensions of every known religion. It is therefore not limited to Judaism or even monotheism, stretching its boundaries to encompass a kind of universal mysticism. Ultimately, it is due to the detailed exploration of Divine Reality that makes the subject truly universal.

Typically interpreted as Jewish mysticism or, in some cases, Western mysticism, Kabbalah—primarily Theoretical and Meditative—bears the closest similarity to a form of Eastern mysticism called "Sufism", which refers to the mystical dimensions of Islam. The similarities between the two range from the Unity of God—described in Kabbalah as *"Shema Yisrael"*, and in Sufism as *"Tawheed"*—to the use of music in meditation—the famous dance meditation in Ecstatic Kabbalah is strikingly similar to the *"Sema"* of the Mevlevi Sufi Order—as far as sharing the same philosophy regarding the realization of Absolute Truth—experienced in Kabbalah through a complete nullification of the ego, similar to a process called *"Fanaa"* and *"Baqaa"* in Sufism, which is the *"annihilation of the self"* in order to live in a state of Divine consciousness (*"subsistence through God"*).

The intimacy between the two mystical schools of thought can also be recognized from their etymological correspondence, with certain words evoking the same nuance and pronunciation—such as *"Cheshk"* in Hebrew, used in Kabbalah to describe passionate Love for God, similar to the Arabic *"Ishq"* which is used in Sufism to describe the ecstasy of Divine Love.

Indeed similar parallels can also be drawn between Kabbalah and the mystical dimensions of Christianity, particularly regarding the concept of the Holy Trinity—which is depicted in Kabbalah through the *Tree of Life,* with the spirit of the Divine Infinite flowing through it. The two also share a good part of their eschatological beliefs, specifically since they interpret the end of time as the Messianic Age—a belief also common to Islam. These numerous connections between the three monotheistic religions ultimately reiterate the oneness of their message, conveyed more so through mystical discourse as it blurs the line between the real and unreal.

The universality of Kabbalah goes beyond the

limitations of monotheism, however, especially in its exploration of *Shekhinah* the Divine Feminine, known by different names in Hinduism and Shamanism—the former being a polytheistic faith and the latter, based heavily on ideas of pantheism. Additionally, the Kabbalistic concept of the Messianic Age in relation to *Shekhinah* is often likened to the dawning of the Aquarian Age in astrology, which is described in Shamanism as the awakening of the Divine Feminine, akin to the Golden Age of the Mayans.

Furthermore, the idea of the ten *sefirot* bears a striking resemblance to the system of *Chakras,* discussed at length in Hinduism and Buddhism. *Chakras* symbolize energy centers within the body, channeling the lifeforce through the mind, body and soul. This echoes the Kabbalistic doctrine of the ten *sefirot* which correspond to the different levels of the human Soul—each representing Divine emanations. In all three schools of thought, experiencing spiritual harmony is the ultimate goal. In Hinduism and Buddhism, for instance, the *chakras* must coexist in balance in order to reach true enlightenment or *Nirvana*—likewise in the Kabbalistic tradition, the five levels of the Soul must unify with the five Higher Realms to experience Divine Union.

After delving into some of the basic teachings of Kabbalah, it is easy to see that traditional Kabbalists encourage a thorough understanding of ancient Hebrew for the purpose of clear communication. After all, the most outstanding feature of this belief system is arguably its extensive focus on the numerological and astrological significance of ancient writings. With a wealth of esoteric knowledge possibly descending from Adam himself—knowledge that has been preserved, studied and internalized for over centuries—it is no wonder that the modern world is showing a renewed interest in Kabbalah.

Although the popularity of Kabbalah Centers has taken away much of the exclusivity that was once attached to this mystical tradition, it is important to keep in mind that the essence of Kabbalah lies in faith, and those who attempt to use its teachings to heal the world are thus considered to be carriers of this faith. It is this underlying belief that binds together Kabbalah with a number of world religions, reiterating the need to overlook each other's differences and instead, view everything, including ourselves, as an extension of the *Ein Sof*—the Divine Infinite—who is ultimately the only Reality that exists.

Symbols of *Kabbalah*

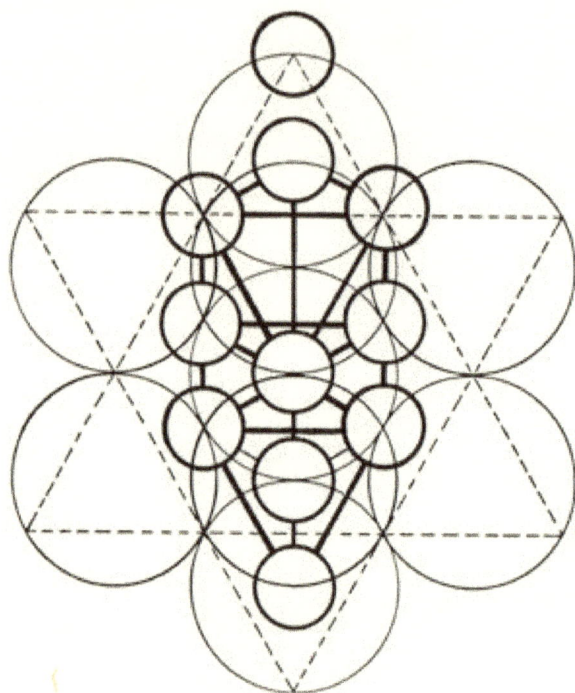

Kabbalah

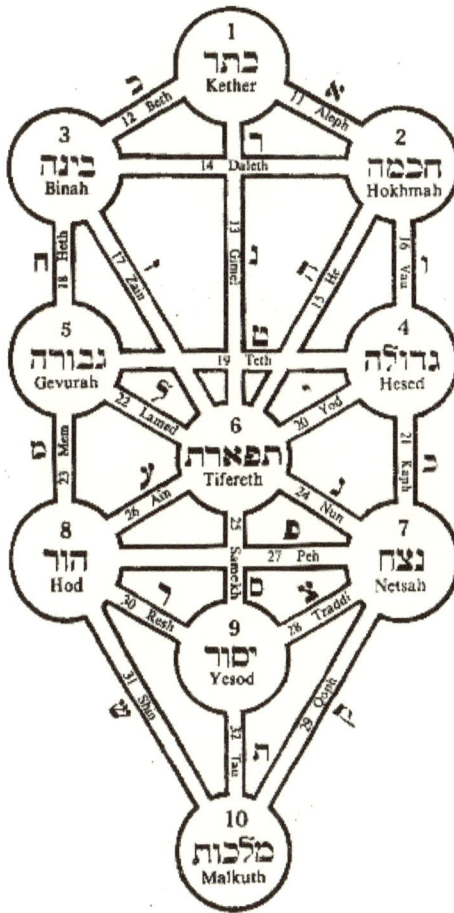

105

Oracle Claretta Pam

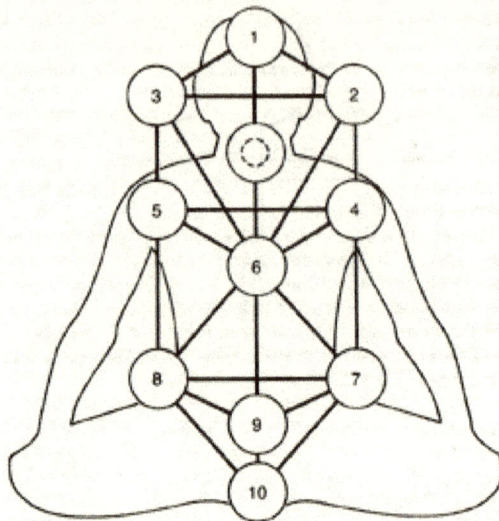

Statement of Faith for the Universal Life Church Monastery of Massachusetts

God or your higher power is holy and calls us to be a holy people.

God or your higher power, who is holy, has abundant and steadfast love for us. God or your higher power 's holy love is revealed to us in the life and teachings, death and resurrection of Jesus Christ, our Savior and Lord. God or your higher power continues to work, giving life, hope and salvation through the indwelling of the Holy Spirit, drawing us into God or your higher powers own holy, loving life. God or your higher power transforms us, delivering us from sin, idolatry, bondage, and self-centeredness to love and serve God or your higher power, others, and to be stewards of creation. Thus, we are renewed in the image of God or your higher power as revealed in Jesus Christ.

Apart from God or your higher power, no one is holy. Holy people are set apart for God or your higher power 's purpose in the world. Empowered by the Holy Spirit, holy people live and love like Jesus Christ. Holiness is both gift and response, renewing and transforming, personal and communal, and ethical. The holy people of God or your higher power follow Jesus Christ in engaging all the cultures of the world and drawing all peoples to God or your higher power.

Holy people are not legalistic or judgmental. They do not pursue an exclusive, private state of being better than others. Holiness is not flawlessness but the fulfillment of God or your higher power 's intention for us. The pursuit of holiness can never cease because love can never be exhausted.

God or your higher power wants us to be, think, speak, and act in the world in a spiritual manner. We invite all to embrace God or your higher power 's call to:

- be filled with all the fullness of God or your higher power;
- live lives that are devout, pure, and reconciled, thereby being an agent of transformation in the world;
- live as a faithful covenant people, building accountable community, growing up, embodying the spirit of God or your higher power 's law in holy love;
- exercise for the common good an effective array of ministries and callings, according to the diversity of the gifts of the Holy Spirit;
- practice compassionate ministries, solidarity with the poor, advocacy for equality, justice, reconciliation, and peace; and
- care for the earth, God or your higher power 's gift in trust to us, working in faith, hope, and confidence for the healing and care of all creation.

By the grace of God or your higher power, let us covenant together to be a holy people.

May this call impel us to rise to this vision of Spiritual mission:
- Preach the transforming message of spirituality
- Teach the principles of love and forgiveness;
- Embody lives that reflect honesty and togetherness;
- Lead in engaging with the cultures of the world; and
- Partner with others to multiply its effect for the reconciliation of all things.

For this we live and labor to the glory of God or your higher power.

Formation of our ministry: the Universal Life Church Monastery of Massachusetts

...ordination is a personal calling by God to minister others. I received my calling on several occasions. I didn't understand why at those times. The first was in May 1990. The second time was in May 1998- at this time, I was going through a difficult period in a marriage and prayed for guidance. In May 2004 is was finishing my studies to receive an MBA and felt like my life was not as full as it could be. This last time, in May 2010, I felt as though many people were always turning to me for advice and comfort and I felt at peace with myself and extremely happy. I am ready to spread my knowledge and his word to all that will listen. Please join me.

ABOUT THE AUTHOR

Oracle Claretta Pam was ordained by the
Universal Life Church Monastery
headquartered in Seattle, WA. Oracle Pam
believes that ultimately we are all one. The path
chosen to spirituality is available to all that seek
it. She is an Interdenominational Oracle that
performs ministerial functions and offers
services that include: weddings, civil unions,
baptisms, naming ceremonies, life coach
services, private ministerial services, house
blessings, hospital visitations and funerals. The
Oracle is the author of several divinity books
and a Guide to Divinity that covers more than
30 religions, belief systems and faiths.

Oracle Claretta Pam

FIND US ONLINE

https://twitter.com/ULCMM

https://www.facebook.com/ULCMM

http://ulcmm.blogspot.com/

http://ministers.themonastery.org/
profile/OracleCPam

http://ulcmm.com

UNIVERSAL LIFE
CHURCH MONASTERY OF
MASSACHUSETTS
We are all people of an equal existence

For membership inquiries
please see us online at
http://ulcmm.com

Kabbalah

Oracle Claretta Pam

Kabbalah

Other forthcoming books available by Oracle Claretta Pam

Agnosticism Atheism Non-Religion
Bahai Faith
Buddhism
Cao Dai
Catholicism
Christianity
Confucianism
Hinduism
Humanism
Islam
Jainism
Jehovas Witnesses
Juche North Korea
Judaism
Natural Law
Neopaganism
New Age
Primal Faith
Primal Indigenous
Rastafarianism
Scientology
Shinto
Sikhism
Spiritism
Taoism
Tarahumara Beliefs
Tenrikyo
The Occult
African Traditional - Diasporic
Unificationism
Unitarian Universalism
Zoroastrianism

Oracle Claretta Pam

Oracle Claretta Pam

Kabbalah

Kabbalah

Oracle Claretta Pam

Kabbalah

Oracle Claretta Pam

Kabbalah

_____
_____
_____
_____
_____
_____
_____
_____
_____
_____
_____
_____
_____
_____
_____
_____
_____
_____
_____
_____
_____

Kabbalah

Oracle Claretta Pam

Oracle Claretta Pam

Oracle Claretta Pam

Kabbalah

Oracle Claretta Pam

Kabbalah

Kabbalah

Oracle Claretta Pam

Kabbalah

Kabbalah

_____

_____

_____

_____

_____

_____

_____

_____

_____

_____

_____

_____

_____

_____

_____

_____

_____

_____

_____

_____

_____

_____

_____

_____

Oracle Claretta Pam

Oracle Claretta Pam

Kabbalah

Oracle Claretta Pam

Kabbalah

Oracle Claretta Pam

Kabbalah

Oracle Claretta Pam

Kabbalah

Oracle Claretta Pam

Kabbalah

Oracle Claretta Pam

Kabbalah

Oracle Claretta Pam

Kabbalah

Oracle Claretta Pam

Kabbalah

Oracle Claretta Pam

Oracle Claretta Pam

Oracle Claretta Pam

Kabbalah

Kabbalah

Oracle Claretta Pam

Kabbalah

Oracle Claretta Pam

Oracle Claretta Pam

Oracle Claretta Pam

Kabbalah

Oracle Claretta Pam

Oracle Claretta Pam

Oracle Claretta Pam

Kabbalah

Oracle Claretta Pam

Oracle Claretta Pam

Kabbalah

Oracle Claretta Pam

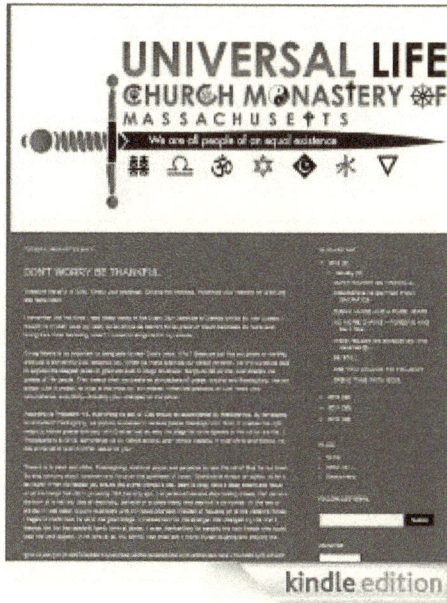

.99 cents per month

Kindle Blogs are auto-delivered wirelessly to your Kindle and updated throughout the day so you can stay current.

It's risk free - this Kindle Blog subscription starts with a 14-day free trial. You can cancel at any time during the free trial period. If you enjoy your subscription, do nothing and it will automatically continue at the regular price.

Subscribe today at
http://www.amazon.com/gp/product/B00B4ICF0U

Something for Everyone.

Embassy™ Alligator Embossed Burgundy Genuine Leather Bible Cover. This leather bible cover features a zippered main pocket, hand strap, pen holder inside, self-closing front pocket, and additional zippered front pocket with cross zipper-pull.
Measures 10" x 7" x 2".

Item#: LULBIBLE3
Weight: 0.55 Pounds
List Price $26.95

20% of all orders will be donated to ULCMM scholarships and programs. Just place ULCMM in the memo section of your order.

Order online at http://groupglobal.net

ADVERTISEMENT

Innovative Publishers

SACREDVISION
PRESS

Kabbalah

www.ingramcontent.com/pod-product-compliance
Lightning Source LLC
Chambersburg PA
CBHW021225090426
42740CB00006B/381